The Wisdom
of Donald Trump

Compiled by E. McSquare

Dedication

To all those who have sought leadership since January 20, 2017 but who have found only obfuscation, division and that newest of political protections – alternate facts and realities.

The Wisdom of Donald Trump

Table of Contents

(See Index)

Foreward

Also known as:
preface, introduction, prologue, preamble, opening remarks, opening statement, preliminary matter front matter, forward matter; etc., etc., etc.;

especially helpful when written by someone who is well known and who is perhaps also famous as a writer.

In response to the title of this book none of my contacts was available to write this material.

E. McSquare
August, 2019

The Wisdom of Donald Trump

Other related volumes:

Vol. 2 The Wisdom of Donald Trump (Condensed)

Vol. 3 The Wisdom of Donald Trump (Expanded)

The Wisdom of Donald Trump

The Wisdom of Donald Trump

The Wisdom of Donald Trump

The Wisdom of Donald Trump

The Wisdom of Donald Trump

The Wisdom of Donald Trump

The Wisdom of Donald Trump

The Wisdom of Donald Trump

The Wisdom of Donald Trump

The Wisdom of Donald Trump

The Wisdom of Donald Trump

The Wisdom of Donald Trump

The Wisdom of Donald Trump

The Wisdom of Donald Trump

The Wisdom of Donald Trump

The Wisdom of Donald Trump

The Wisdom of Donald Trump

The Wisdom of Donald Trump

The Wisdom of Donald Trump

The Wisdom of Donald Trump

The Wisdom of Donald Trump

The Wisdom of Donald Trump

The Wisdom of Donald Trump

The Wisdom of Donald Trump

The Wisdom of Donald Trump

The Wisdom of Donald Trump

The Wisdom of Donald Trump

The Wisdom of Donald Trump

The Wisdom of Donald Trump

The Wisdom of Donald Trump

The Wisdom of Donald Trump

The Wisdom of Donald Trump

The Wisdom of Donald Trump

The Wisdom of Donald Trump

The Wisdom of Donald Trump

The Wisdom of Donald Trump

The Wisdom of Donald Trump

The Wisdom of Donald Trump

The Wisdom of Donald Trump

The Wisdom of Donald Trump

The Wisdom of Donald Trump

The Wisdom of Donald Trump

The Wisdom of Donald Trump

The Wisdom of Donald Trump

The Wisdom of Donald Trump

The Wisdom of Donald Trump

The Wisdom of Donald Trump

The Wisdom of Donald Trump

The Wisdom of Donald Trump

The Wisdom of Donald Trump

The Wisdom of Donald Trump

The Wisdom of Donald Trump

The Wisdom of Donald Trump

The Wisdom of Donald Trump

The Wisdom of Donald Trump

The Wisdom of Donald Trump

The Wisdom of Donald Trump

The Wisdom of Donald Trump

The Wisdom of Donald Trump

The Wisdom of Donald Trump

The Wisdom of Donald Trump

The Wisdom of Donald Trump

The Wisdom of Donald Trump

The Wisdom of Donald Trump

The Wisdom of Donald Trump

The Wisdom of Donald Trump

The Wisdom of Donald Trump

The Wisdom of Donald Trump

The Wisdom of Donald Trump

The Wisdom of Donald Trump

The Wisdom of Donald Trump

The Wisdom of Donald Trump

The Wisdom of Donald Trump

The Wisdom of Donald Trump

The Wisdom of Donald Trump

The Wisdom of Donald Trump

The Wisdom of Donald Trump

The Wisdom of Donald Trump

The Wisdom of Donald Trump

The Wisdom of Donald Trump

The Wisdom of Donald Trump

The Wisdom of Donald Trump

The Wisdom of Donald Trump

The Wisdom of Donald Trump

The Wisdom of Donald Trump

The Wisdom of Donald Trump

The Wisdom of Donald Trump

The Wisdom of Donald Trump

The Wisdom of Donald Trump

The Wisdom of Donald Trump

The Wisdom of Donald Trump

The Wisdom of Donald Trump

The Wisdom of Donald Trump

The Wisdom of Donald Trump

The Wisdom of Donald Trump

The Wisdom of Donald Trump

The Wisdom of Donald Trump

The Wisdom of Donald Trump

The Wisdom of Donald Trump

The Wisdom of Donald Trump

The Wisdom of Donald Trump

The Wisdom of Donald Trump

The Wisdom of Donald Trump

The Wisdom of Donald Trump

The Wisdom of Donald Trump

Index

(see Table of Contents)

THE WISDOM OF DONALD TRUMP

"This is a tough hurricane. One of the wettest we've ever seen from the standpoint of water"

"Actually, throughout my life, my two greatest assets have been mental stability, and being, like, really smart."

"...President of the United States (on my first try). I think that would qualify as not smart, but genius ….and a very stable genius at that!"

Compiled by E.McSquare
2019
Volume 1

www.ingramcontent.com/pod-product-compliance
Lightning Source LLC
Chambersburg PA
CBHW062143280526
45788CB00001B/281